FORMULA AWESOME

Formula To Being Happy

Mousam Chatterjee

ISBN 978-93-5559-048-0

Published in India 2021 by Pencil

A brand of
One Point Six Technologies Pvt. Ltd.
123, Building J2, Shram Seva Premises,
Wadala Truck Terminal, Wadala (E)
Mumbai 400037, Maharashtra, INDIA
E connect@thepencilapp.com
W www.thepencilapp.com

Author biography

Mousam Chatterjee is the owner of Animation Door Studios. He wrote 4 non-fiction books which are available for free to all to help and grow others. He has completed his graduation in animation filmmaking at the age of 21 from 'Whistling Wood International'. He has acted in many highly regarded short films, and after successfully automating his online business he started his acting career by learning through theatres. Everyone used to laugh at him due to his extraordinary dreams and the path to follow them but all of this he achieved at the age of 22 and sometimes he teaches many people about self-help and growth in a form of online coaching.

CONTENTS

Acknowledgements

'Formula Awesome' has been composed for data purposes as it were. Each work has been made to make this digital book as complete and precise as could be expected. Notwithstanding, there might be botches in typography or content. Additionally, Formula Awesome gives data simply up to the distributing date. Along these lines, this book ought to be utilized as an aide - not as a definitive source.

The motivation behind Formula Awesome is to teach. The creator and the distributor doesn't warrant that the data contained in Formula Awesome is finished and will not be answerable for any blunders or on the other hand exclusions. The creator and distributor will have neither obligation nor obligation to any individual or element regarding any misfortune or on the other hand, harm caused or affirmed to be caused straightforwardly or in a roundabout way by Formula Awesome.

This book is the story of the awesome formula- what I tried, what I learned. Your Formula will look different than mine, but it's the rare person who can't benefit from Formula Awesome. I hope that reading the account of formula awesome will encounter you start your own. Whenever you read this, Whatever you are, and wherever you are, you are in the right place

GETTING STARTED

We carry on with life-giving a valiant effort to arrive at our fantasies and our objectives. We feel that whenever we've made progress, we'll, at last, be

glad and content with the world. This might be valid. Nonetheless, the basic reality is that not every person will wind up successful. Just a little minority will arrive at the zenith of abundance and power.

The majority of us will get stuck carrying on with mediocre lives.

In this way, the question is, does that mean just a little level of individuals are going to carry on with cheerful lives? Are the rich, powerful and successful the only ones with the right to feel awesome in life?

The appropriate response is, luckily, no. You want neither cash nor

the ability to have a cheerful and satisfying life. After all, feeling awesome is a state of mind.

You can have all the cash on the planet and still be unhappy. On the opposite side of the coin, you can have no common belongings yet, carry on with an extremely glad life.

In this in-depth guide on awesomeness, you will discover that your joy isn't reliant upon cash, profession, or status throughout everyday life. It begins with you.

Chapter1

The road to Awesomeness

"The most simple things can bring the most happiness." -Izabella Scorupco

We as a whole have various meanings of happiness. What may satisfy you may not be a wellspring of satisfaction for others. What others call their wellspring of happiness and satisfaction, possibly a wellspring of scorn for you.

For example, many might say their bliss comes from their families and their great well-being. For other people, it very well may be their positions and their professions. For some's purposes, it's their abundance and their social remaining locally. For over a couple of individuals, scrumptious food and beverages light them up like no other. Also, the list continues.

All things considered, specialists have since a long time ago bantered on a solitary meaning of bliss. This is because there are extremely many elements that affect and add to an individual's bliss. The agreement, notwithstanding, is that "satisfaction is the condition of being glad."

I realize this definition appears to be somewhat obscure, however, the fact is that bliss is a psychological expression that mirrors the scope of feelings you experience consistently. It characterizes how you view your life, that is, regardless of whether you're fulfilled or unsatisfied with your satisfaction. Assuming you're disappointed, then, at that point, it implies you're upset. In any case, on the off chance that you are, then, at that point, bravo!

Presently the thing is because somebody's cheerful doesn't mean they will be insusceptible to negative feelings. Nothing can be further from reality. Cheerful individuals experience preliminaries and difficulties, however, they manage these uniquely in contrast to troubled individuals would. This is the thing that separates them from the remainder of the populace.

Glad individuals aren't dissuaded without any problem. They're less vulnerable to negative feelings. They don't permit others to mistreat them. Their satisfaction is infectious, and individuals normally float towards them. You'd know a truly cheerful individual when you meet them. They can in a real sense light up a room just by being in it.

Regardless of your meaning of satisfaction is, this straightforward truth remains: we would all be able to utilize some more bliss in our lives. The world will be a vastly improved spot to live in assuming that everybody on this planet transmits joy.

Chapter 2

Figure Out Why You're Unhappy

"Unhappiness is not knowing what we want and killing ourselves to get it." -

At the point when you're continually feeling the blues and you can't recollect the last time you've felt cheerful and free, then, at that point, you want to sort out why at the earliest opportunity. Stalling out in a troubled state is not great for any rational individual as misery can rapidly twist into discouragement. Ideally, it isn't past the point of no return. The following are a couple of inquiries you can pose to yourself to sort out what's causing your misery.

Is it accurate to say that you are doing what you need to do?

Pose this vital inquiry. Assuming you reply "no," then, at that point, what are you doing about it? It is safe to say that you are making any strides towards the work or vocation you need? Or then again, do you feel like you're caught in a day work you don't especially like, however you stay in this is because it takes care of the bills?

For some individuals, this is a typical problem. They know they're not content with their present positions, yet they stay in it year in and year out. They dislike it, however, they feel like they have no other decision. Throughout some undefined time frame, their day occupations become their solace zone. They become terrified of seeking after their interests. Assuming you're one of them, then, at that point, you want to sort out how you can free yourself to seek after your inclinations and your interests throughout everyday life.

In the first place, you likely had very little said in the matter. Your folks presumably didn't uphold your fantasy to become an artist or an expert competitor or a craftsman. They've presumably heard harrowing tales of individuals who sought after their interests and wound up ravenous and destitute. Since you're as well

reluctant to defy your folks, you do their offering and work at a work you disdain.

Assuming that this story sounds natural, or then again in case you're caught in this

position, then, at that point, it's an ideal opportunity to take care of business. Can you not view it as a

method for pursuing your enthusiasm? What steps would you say you are taking to free yourself of this snare?

Your answers will ideally assist you with seeing the light, so you can at long last beginning seeking after the profession that will satisfy you.

Are your thoughts making you unhappy?

You have a say concerning what continues in your brain, that is, you

have a decision about the sort of contemplations you permit to go through your mind. You can decide to think emphatically, or you can pick the inverse. Assuming you pick the last option, then, at that point, it will make you troubled.

You can without much of a stretch advise yourself to quit thinking negative musings.

Yet, this is more difficult than one might expect. We can knock our heads all we need, and the negative musings will in any case proceed in the foundation. This is in a real sense why certain individuals go off the deep end. They hear voices, and they can't quit paying attention to it regardless they do.

Representation assumes a crucial part in beating negative musings.

But at the same time be mindful and focus on your contemplations.

Here is a stunt you can attempt at this moment: Every time you discover yourself thinking adversely, advise yourself to stop. Take a full breath and envision your entire body's covered in oil and the cynicism's sliding off of you. With the antagonism expelled from your brain, you would then be able to allow your positive considerations to dominate.

Are you aiming for perfection?

There are heaps of things you can be focusing on – flawlessness isn't one of them. Why? Since when you put out flawlessness as your definitive objective, you're unavoidably setting yourself up for disappointment. In addition to any disappointment, however a calamitous one at that, particularly assuming you give it your everything.

Rather than flawlessness, target something more sensible, like

greatness, for example. It's still higher up on the accomplishment

scale, however, at any rate, it's more feasible. Not so much as one of us is awesome, so why focus on flawlessness?

Flawlessness is, to put it obtusely, misrepresented. At the point when you focus on flawlessness, you set a bar so high that when you make a solitary, little slip-up, it can cause all that you've buckled down for to disintegrate.

At the point when you focus on greatness, notwithstanding, you give yourself a battling opportunity to succeed. You're not going to be frightened to go

out there and make a nitwit of yourself since you know your odds of making it are great. You utilize your slip-ups and your disappointments as learning encounters.

Also the other advantage of focusing on greatness? You've generally got some more space to develop! You can be the best entertainer at work, in school, or your game, and still, have the chance to do a far superior occupation sometime later.

Whenever you've sorted out why you're miserable, you'll have the option to push ahead lastly be on the way to making bliss in your life.

Chapter 3

Be Grateful And Be Appreciative

"Time and health are two precious assets that we don't recognize and appreciate until they have been depleted." - Denis Waitley

At the point when your despondency is consuming your spirit, and you think all that you have will squander, reconsider. Check out you. What do you see? What do you smell? What do you hear? When was the last time you took a gander at the sky? Like, truly checked out it? Would you be able to see the value in the sound of leaves stirring in the breeze? Or on the other hand the vibe of grass on your exposed feet?

Presently, envision having every one of these detracted from you. Envision losing your vision, your hearing, your feeling of touch, your sense

of taste, and your feeling of smell. Pause for a minute to ponder what you're passing up.

Envision spending the remainder of your existence without your faculties as a whole. It's incredibly hard, right? You'd most likely be headed to end your life at that moment since life as far as you might be concerned has finished.

Your life won't ever go back again.

Luckily, the above is the only activity. Yet, an incredible one at that. I trust it made you see exactly how inconsequential every one of your concerns is

contrasted with having everything – in a real sense everything – removed

from you.

The following are 10 things you ought to appreciate throughout everyday life:

1. **Life**.

Consistently you awaken, you're given one more rent throughout everyday life. You have another chance to begin your life over again, to make

alters, to have an effect in this world.

Rather than walking during your time like you're conveying the heaviness of the world on your shoulders, attempt to experience every day like it were your last. Every day you live like this will be your greatest day of all time!

2. **Family**.

Regardless of how bustling life gets, always find some time to connect

with your family. Your folks gave life to you, without them

you'll not be anything. Assuming you have kin, figure out how to see the value in them

also. Assuming you have a more distant family, invest quality energy with

them also. Everybody in your family helped mold you to

become the individual you are today.

3. **Friendship**.

Having companions you can depend on is significant. You have

somebody to impart your considerations and your sentiments too. They can work on your life, and similarly, you can assist with enhancing theirs too. Have significant discussions with your companions.

4. **Health**.

Great wellbeing frequently goes unacknowledged. Figure out how to take great care of your body. We're simply reminded to be thankful for our well-being when sickness comes upon us. Indeed, even the smallest agony can burden us extraordinarily, more so genuine and basic diseases.

5. **Love**.

Regardless of whether it's heartfelt or non-romantic love, self or caring adoration, the saying "love drives everything and everyone" holds a lot of shrewdness. Love makes you wake up. It propels you to get up ahead of schedule, to stroll with a spring in your progression, to grin and snicker all the more regularly, and numerous other positive changes.

6. **Laughter**.

There's a ton of things to giggle about in this life, regardless of how terrible you believe it's become. Chuckling has a lot of advantages, counting makes you better. At the point when you snicker, you lessen your feelings of anxiety. At the point when you share a snicker with another individual, you promptly feel a bond with that individual.

7. **Tears**.

Tears might be seen adversely, yet it's not too terrible. At times, tears are fundamental. It helps put things in viewpoint. It assists you with liking life and chuckling even more.

8. **Nature**.

While there's less of nature now than there was a couple of centuries prior, there's still bounty left to appreciate. Regardless of whether you live in a metropolitan wilderness, you can in any case set aside some effort to respect mother nature. Like the greenness that plants and trees bring. Take a gander at the creatures eating on grass. Notice and be astonished at how nature reclaims what's hers in deserted spots.

9. **Time**.

We don't have a boundless stockpile of time. The second we're conceived, our bodies begin counting down how a lot of time we have left. We don't know precisely when it's going to end, which is the reason we can't give minor issues access life brings us down. How about we partake in the restricted measure of time we have here on this planet.

10. **Yourself**.

Indeed, you. Figure out how to see the value in yourself. You're noticeably flawed, no one is. In any case, you've progressed significantly since your mom gave birth to you. Ponder every one of your triumphs and your disappointments, your expectations, and your fantasies. Then, at that point, contemplate individuals you've met en route, how you've helped them in one way or then again another. Ponder the heritage you will leave behind.

Figure out how to like all that you have in your life – both great furthermore terrible. Eventually, they all meet up to give a novel educational experience that is intended to challenge you and draw out the best in you. At the point when you quit agonizing over everything and start liking each easily overlooked detail throughout everyday life, your bliss will turn into obvious, to yourself, yet to everybody around you, as well.

Chapter 4

Your Comfort Zone Isn't Making You Happy

"Life begins at the end of your comfort zone." - Neale Donald Walsch

Remaining in your usual range of familiarity is similarly pretty much as significant as passing on it every once in a while. Despite mainstream thinking, your usual range of familiarity isn't fixed to a solitary area. It's not limited by actual dividers. Our usual range of familiarity exists in our psyche. So, it ought to be not difficult to receive in return right? Sadly, the appropriate response is "no." It's more confounded than that.

Safe places are called 'solace' which is as it should be. This is because all that falls inside this zone makes us agreeable, we know everything about everything. It doesn't give us any migraines. It doesn't cause us any pressure. It's the place where we for the most part head to the second life turns out to be a lot for us to bear. It's your 'standard thing' climate where you control everything, and you don't realize anything will come out at you and alarm you to no end.

Safe places are all around great. Be that as it may, it turns into something negative when it keeps you away from carrying on with your daily routine how it's intended to be experienced.

Think about a turtle stowing away in its shell. You're the turtle, and the shell is your usual range of familiarity. You need to evaluate a genuinely new thing, however, you're excessively apprehensive. Your companions are requesting that you look at a novel, new thing, and fun, yet you deny it. You consume your whole time on earth

in your shell. That is all you know. Also, you don't get to carry on with life by any means. You're just living inside your shell.

The facts confirm that you can be cheerful inside your usual range of familiarity. Yet, like with most things throughout everyday life, you want to chip away at keeping up with that degree of bliss. Also to do that, you'd need to get out of your safe place.

We should take, for instance, a wedded couple. At the point when you're a love bird, everything appears to be so invigorating, so great. Be that as it may, a couple of months or not many years not too far off, you understand that both of you have become very all right with the existence you've made, and you're as of now not cheerful. You're done filling in your relationship.

You do the same things over and over, every day of the week. There's no assortment in your everyday schedule or your marriage. Despondency begins to develop. To battle this, you'd need to accomplish something strange. Both you and your companion are underestimating each other, and you should buckle down on fulfilling the marriage by and by. Maybe you can both take up moving illustrations, or you plan something gutsy on your days off. Rediscover one another by leaving your usual ranges of familiarity behind.

Here are alternate ways you can break out of your usual range of familiarity:

• **Remind yourself of your dreams**

Try not to allow your solace to zone drag you down. You know what you need where it counts inside, yet you're excessively scared of the multitude of dangers and the questions en route. A practical technique for following your dreams, and limiting the dangers, is by arranging. Have a strong arrangement on how you will get from point A (where you are present) to point B (your huge dream).

On the off chance that you can separate it into achievements and scaled-down objectives, it will be far and away superior. Along these lines, you're not going to feel like David following Goliath.

Each time you accomplish an achievement, it brings you one bit nearer to your objectives. Simply relax. Have a day-by-day, week after week, or month-to-month objective, and you will not understand how far you've left your usual range of familiarity behind!

• **Be brave and face your fears**

Because you're leaving your usual range of familiarity behind doesn't mean you will be entering a place of extreme peril. The rest of the world might be turbulent, however, in case you invest sufficient energy in it, you'll become familiar with it's not downright terrible. There's a similarity to arrange there. You simply need to wake up and perceive the signs and the examples. When arranging your extraordinary departure, ask yourself what your biggest fears are and then, at that point, sort out how you can battle these fears. Assuming you're anxious about open talking, maybe this is because you disdain the possibility of individuals snickering at you.

To face your dread, have a go at considering it along these lines:

you have a very significant message to share, and the main way individuals are going to find out with regards to it is by assuming that you go out there and tell them. In any case, they're going to carry on with their lives in happy obliviousness. Additionally, you can say to yourself that maybe 50% of your crowd is in something similar boat as you. They're similarly as scared of public talking as you are.

Along these lines, your concerns aren't all that bad. Whatever your fear is, break it down until you can see exactly how absurd and insignificant everything is in the grand plan of things!

• Learn a new skill

Learning a new skill in this day and age is an absolute necessity. Managers value it, colleagues appreciate it, and the best part is that you're not restricting yourself to a solitary skill. New skills will open up an entirely new world for you. Indeed, it's most probably going to take a little time, however assuming you continue to do the same things over and over, you're eventually going to get abandoned. Assuming you want to succeed throughout everyday life, you want to get as many relevant skills as conceivable. In short, you can never have an excess of skill.

• Strike up a conversation

At the point when we were kids, our parents advised us to never talk to strangers. Be that as it may, it doesn't have to carry on to our adult lives. We're better informed, and we're savvy enough to recognize whom we ought to be

avoiding and whom we ought to associate with. Perhaps you've got a new colleague at work. The individual in question is by all accounts the timid sort. Instead of stowing away in your workspace, go say "Hey!" and present yourself. That individual will appreciate your graciousness and you'll end up having a happy outlook on yourself.

Chapter 5

Embrace And Welcome Change

"Change will not come if we wait for some other person or some other time. We are the ones we've been waiting for. We are the change that we seek."

- Barack Obama

You need to feel awesome, isn't that so? Then, at that point, take the necessary steps so you can encounter genuine bliss! That's all there is to it. In any case, nothing at any point plays out that effectively throughout everyday life. It's to such an extent simpler to say you'll change than to do it. There are two sorts of progress: positive and negative. It may not continuously be apparent from the beginning, that is, you don't know whether the change you are accepting will prompt great outcomes or terrible outcomes. Now and then, you want to go out on a limb and do what needs to be done.

When dealing with change, you can initiate it or you can wait for it to happen. The beneficial thing is assuming you initiate it, you're in a greatly improved situation to control it rather than simply reacting to it. It's also easier for you to adapt to the change because you're anticipating it. As such, you're not going to feel like it came unexpectedly and sucker-punched you.

However change is regularly painted negatively by naysayers, there are a lot of advantages to embracing change. Here are some of them:

• You can discover new opportunities

The facts confirm that there are opportunities all over the place. At the point when you've braced yourself to embrace change, it's easier for you to uncover secret opportunities. Certain individuals may even say, the chance will reveal itself to you. This is because when you embrace change, you open your eyes as well. Where every other person is fleeing from the change, you're walking towards it with eyes open. This makes it easier for you to spot new opportunities.

• You'll grow as a person

Failure to embrace change means you will get stuck doing the same things over and over again. There's no space for you to develop and improve personally. You can change your negative propensities and supplant them with new ones. At the point when you move from one spot to another, you expand your viewpoint. You adjust to your new environmental factors, and you learn new things. Frequently, the best way to advance is by greeting change wholeheartedly.

• You'll discover your strengths (and weaknesses)

Tolerating and accepting change will allow you to discover your strengths and even your weaknesses. For example, assuming you get allotted into a new job at your specific employment, you might understand that you're more qualified for the new job than your old one, and your efficiency will be at an all-time high. Similarly, assuming that you make a plunge into a new business, you'll discover the regions you're great at and where you're in an ideal situation designating to somebody more qualified and more skilled than you are.

• You'll learn new ways to solve problems

At the point when you don't avoid transforming, you'll eventually sort out new ways to solve problems. Getting presented with new conditions assists you with breaking new ground. So, change can draw out your inventiveness. It empowers you to look for new arrangements all the more effectively and successfully. Be that as it may, in case you would not acknowledge the change, in any case, you'd be stuck investigating the standard, worn-out problems.

Making an existence of joy implies accepting change. It implies getting out of your usual range of familiarity. Ask yourself, what would you be able to change in your life right since will prompt your definitive bliss?

Do you have to change occupations? Do you want to take up a new leisure activity? Do you think moving to another city or another nation is essential for you to accomplish joy? Just you know the response to this inquiry.

The significant thing to recall is that chasing and embracing change ought to be on the first spot on your list if you truly need to accomplish genuine satisfaction.

Chapter 6

Say Goodbye To Your Bad Habits

"The only proper way to eliminate bad habits is to replace them with good

ones." - Jerome Hines

Assuming you need to make the existence of satisfaction, then, at that point, it's basic that you begin chipping away at disposing of your negative propensities, and supplanting them with positive ones. In any case, doing this isn't quite so straightforward as it sounds. This is because unfortunate quirks require some investment to construct. It doesn't occur out of the blue. All things being equal, it happens throughout some undefined time frame until it gets somewhat where you do the propensity out of repetition. You don't have to consider it; you take care of business. That is the point at which you realize you've framed a propensity.

Negative quirks have the unfortunate impact of making you despondent over the long haul. Without a doubt, it might present to you some type of fulfillment while you're doing the everyday practice or propensity, however, it won't be useful for you or your wellbeing as time passes by. For instance, smoking. You feel great when you're smoking.

The demonstration of breathing in and breathing out tobacco smoke assists you with diffusing your feelings of anxiety to sensible levels. In any case, on the other side, smoking has a ton of negative incidental effects, particularly on your wellbeing. Long haul impacts of smoking incorporate malignant growth, cerebrum harm, emphysema, tooth rot, thus substantially more. Indeed, even the individuals breathing in your recycled smoke are in danger of these sicknesses, as well. Along these lines, smoking is simply going to bring you transitory fulfillment. Over the long haul, it will kill you.

Presently, ending unfortunate quirks will moreover take some time. You'd need to truly deal with it and have the mindfulness to know at the point when you're doing the propensity. Then, at that point, you want restraint and self-discipline to have the option to end it. The following are a couple of methodologies you can use to assist you with bidding farewell to your negative propensities:

Understand What's Your Trigger

Specialists say propensities have three sections: a trigger or prompt, an everyday practice, lastly, an award. For instance, in a smoker's case, one potential trigger could be eating. After you've eaten, you feel a compelling impulse to smoke. Or then again, it may be the case that pressure is your trigger. At the point when you're anxious, they need to smoke become more grounded.

Knowing what your prompts or triggers are is the initial step to conquering an unfortunate quirk. Concentrate on your unfortunate quirks, dissect when you want to complete them. Assuming you're attempting to stop drinking liquor, then, at that point, quit purchasing liquor. At the point when you're associating with companions, go ahead and let them know you're attempting to stop. If you have great companions, they'll support you and assist you with accomplishing your objectives, so they're not going to offer any liquor to you. If your companions still pressure you to drink, then, at that point, maybe you should begin spending less time with them and observe others who'll be more strong.

Reduce your stress times negative quirks structure because of different stressors in our life. You get the propensity for smoking when you're anxious. You get drinking when you're exhausted or when you have issues at home. You get dawdling when confronted with a pile of work. At the point when you're attempting to beat cutoff times, you drink huge loads of espresso to give yourself a psychological lift.

These are nevertheless a couple of instances of negative quirks that individuals get when they become pushed. In case you end up reacting contrarily to stretch, then, at that point, it's an ideal opportunity to take care of business. How? By making an honest effort to diminish your feelings of anxiety.

Sort out what makes you push, and attempt to track down an approach to stay away from these circumstances to make your feelings of anxiety go down. As a rule, carrying on with a calm life won't be imaginable, so you want to deal with it directly and figure out how to control or deal with your stress.

So, it's imperative to take note that pressure isn't such an awful thing. Truth be told, numerous specialists say some pressure is vital for our lives. It discharges chemicals that trigger our endurance impulses. It assists us with playing out our assignments all the more proficiently and all the more successfully. It possibly turns into something terrible when you let it assume control over your life, that is the point at which you permit yourself to get focused on continually.

Anchor your negative habits to new and positive ones

Perhaps the simplest method for bringing an end to an unfortunate quirk and supplanting it with a positive one is to utilize an 'anchor' framework. This is the way it works: each time you discover yourself beginning to do the negative quirk, you do the enhanced one all things being equal.

For example, you're attempting to end the negative propensity of, say, gnawing your nails. Suppose this negative quirk is set off by pressure. Presently, you additionally need to construct a more sure propensity for perusing or paying attention to moving substances to assist you with growing an individual.

Each time you discover yourself gnawing your nails, you stop and afterward you get a decent book close by and read a couple of pages. Or on the other hand, you can go on YouTube and pay attention to your most loved persuasive speakers. Following half a month of doing this daily practice, you'll have the option to eliminate nail-gnawing from your rundown of negative quirks, and end up additional enlivened and less pushed simultaneously.

List all the reasons why you should quit those habit

There's a motivation behind why negative quirks are called 'terrible.' They have undesired impacts that might show right away. For instance, drinking. You realize that when you drink in abundance, you end up with an awful headache in the first part of the day. You've presumably vomited a couple of times out in the open. Maybe you notice your companions are done welcoming you to get-togethers and gatherings since they're apprehensive you'll have a lot to drink and create a situation.

Record this large number of unfortunate results and use it as your "why" for why you should quit drinking.

Make your depictions as itemized and as realistic as could be expected. Each time you make a mistake and you return to your old ways, look into this rundown and make a guarantee to improve sometime later.

Reevaluate your life from time and time and survey assuming you have any unfortunate quirks passed on that should be halted. You might get some other unfortunate quirks later on, regardless of whether you wind up turning your everyday routine around and experiencing a cheerful presence. That is OK. Nobody's ideal. Simply refocus and work constantly on making yourself a superior individual every day.

Chapter 7

Learn To Love Yourself First

"You can't let someone else lower your self-esteem, because that's what it is - self-esteem. You need to first love yourself before you have anybody else love you." - Winnie Harlow

Adoring yourself is essential to making the existence of satisfaction. This is because you must be really glad and content with the world assuming you love yourself. In like manner, you can't completely cherish someone else on the off chance that you don't see the value in yourself in the first place.

So, how can you say whether you love yourself enough?

The following are a couple of tips:

You love what you see in the mirror

You don't have to have the most excellent or the most attractive face known to man to see the value in your looks. You additionally don't have to have a supermodel's body to say you look attractive. We can't be generally so lucky to win the hereditary lottery. Yet, truly, even those we think to look 'amazing' have uncertainties also.

We believe that making ourselves look wonderful is the best way to like what we find in the mirror. In any case, when we're continually contrasting ourselves with another person, and we're generally spotting blemishes in any event, when there are none, then, at that point, it's never going to stop, right? You'll never be happy with your looks and yourself. You'll generally track down something to condemn.

Without a doubt, restorative innovation might have progressed significantly, and you would now be able to change your actual appearance to your optimal one, yet, at what cost? Corrective specialists don't by and large do free work, so hope to go through a large chunk of change. Sadly, not everybody has that sort of money lying around, so they're left with no decision yet to keep away from the mirror. Be that as it may, do you truly have to do that? The uplifting news is you don't need to.

You simply need to chip away at tolerating yourself for what your identity is, that incorporates your looks. Whether or not you like it, it's the face you were brought into the world with. Figure out how to look past the physical. Sooner or afterward, you'll be agreeable in your skin, and the mirror will at last turn into your companion.

You prioritize yourself above everyone else

Prioritizing on yourself over others is certainly not an indication of narrow-mindedness, it simply implies you love yourself more than others. Nonetheless, assuming you take it to a limit, that is, in case you venture over others to get what you need, then, at that point, it's an alternate story. Yet, in case you're not harming anybody, then, at that point, it's OK.

The issue with a great many people is that they're too reluctant to even think about harming others' sentiments. They follow their folks' desires, their companion's requests. They effectively do homage peer pressure even though they realize what they're being approached to do conflicts with their values.

Surrendering to individuals you like and love is all right, yet don't make it a propensity. Your purported companions can undoubtedly take advantage of your trust. On the off chance that you try not to figure out how to go to bat for yourself and battle for what you accept, they can without much of a stretch control you to do their offering.

Allowing others to mistreat you is not an indication of magnanimity. It's an indication of idiocy, for the absence of a superior word. You're a relaxing person. You have your fantasies, your objectives, your own life to live. Try not to burn through your time satisfying others if you are troubled in the first place. Assuming you need to commit your life to fulfilling others, you should be in a place of adoring yourself completely first.

You take care of your body and your health

Nothing says self-hatred is stronger than allowing your well-being to go to squander. The old banality is valid: your body is your sanctuary. Assuming you don't deal with your body, then, at that point, it implies you're not dealing with your sanctuary.

You don't have to pursue an exercise center participation at this moment. Neither do you want to purchase all-natural food starting from here forward? Dealing with your wellbeing implies focusing on your body and its necessities. Make a propensity for eating quality food what's more quit taking care of yourself with low-quality nourishment. Quit doing whatever degenerates your body. Things, like smoking and drinking, and ingesting medications, aren't cool. Certainly, these may give you a momentary explosion of joy, however over the long haul, you're going to experience for sure. Figure out how to pay attention to your body. At the point when you're anxious and tired, take a rest. Go home for the day. Disappear for the end of the week. Once in a while, you may likewise need to not do anything by any stretch of the imagination for the entire day. Marathon watching Netflix isn't great assuming you do it consistently. Yet, if it's simply one time each week or one time per month, then, at that point, it shouldn't be an issue, particularly assuming that it assists you with taking your brain off upsetting things like work.

Give yourself some space to move around. As the adage goes, a lack of work-life balance will drive a person crazy. You get to have some good times, yet you likewise give your body a genuinely necessary break from the rushing about of your everyday schedule.

Chapter 8

Build Positive Relationships

"Treasure your relationships, not your possessions." - Anthony J. D'Angelo

Material belongings can sure fulfill you, yet not close to so much assuming you share those belongings with individuals you love and regard. All things considered, we are designed to flourish in human contact and connections.

From the second you were conceived, you had a moment relationship with your folks, kin, and more distant family individuals. At the point when you went to class, you had colleagues. At the point when you went to work, you had associates and collaborators. Etc. You will go through your whole life constructing and keeping up with kinships with many individuals.

Sadly, not all connections will be cheerful. You'll presumably have your reasonable part of poisonous associations with individuals around you; this incorporates your nearest relatives and companions.

Assuming you need to carry on with a cheerful life, then, at that point, you want to invest less and less energy with these harmful people. In case you can stand to remove them from your life through and through, then, at that point, do it. It very well might be hard, yet assuming it's overall a good thing, that is, carrying on with your existence without them will fulfill you, then, at that point, take the plunge. Some of the time, total separation is all you want to push your satisfaction meter from void to full.

At the point when you're with the right sort of individuals (the great kind), your bliss will be out of this world. You'll be more joyful, more roused, and bound to be content. Investing your energy with great individuals will be the feature of your day or even your week or month on the off chance that you don't invest close to as much time with them as you'd like.

The following are a couple of ways of beginning structure positive associations with individuals around you:

Get to know other people

In case you're the timid kind, then, at that point, it's an ideal opportunity to begin escaping your shell. Step up to the plate and begin conversing with individuals. Say something decent and attempt to assemble affinity, and check whether you can get a discussion rolling. Some likely would need to be left alone. However, for a great many people, having another person start the discussion frees them once again from their shell, as well. Appreciate making another companion!

Be more understanding

Whether or not you like it, probably the most effective way you can fabricate associations with others is to be seriously understanding. Take a stab at being receptive when meeting new individuals. All things considered, we as a whole have our disparities. We are exceptional people with our mentalities, our convictions, our societies. At the point when you're seriously understanding, you can without much of a stretch envision yourself in the other individual's shoes to realize where they're coming from.

Be a good listener

Listening is far beyond being somebody's sounding board. Pay attention to what the individual is saying and attempt to get what's really being said, rather than simply gesturing absentmindedly. Great audience members make extraordinary companions; it shows you genuinely care about the other individual.

Be a decent communicator

A ton of issues can emerge when correspondence lines get crossed. This is the reason it's fundamental to foster your relational abilities. It's so natural to accept everybody gets what you're saying, when the truth is told, they're misinterpreting it.

Relationships can rapidly turn sour along these lines. You're saying a certain something, however, the other individual is deciphering it in an altogether unique way.

Positive connections accomplish such a great deal for us. The more certain connections you have, the more joyful you will for the most part be. Glad connections construct our confidence and assist us with making a halfhearted effort of life in a more sure state. This, thus, has a helpful impact of causing you to appreciate life more.

Chapter 9

The Right Choices In Life

"Our lives are a total of the choices we have made." - Wayne Dyer

We settle on choices for the day. Most don't need a lot of thinking; you simply know precisely the thing you will do. In any case, by and large, you want to pause and set aside some effort to think about your choice where you gauge the advantages and disadvantages of the relative multitude of choices accessible to you. At the point when the stakes are higher, and you remain to lose something significant, settling on the ideal decision is of most extreme significance.

Losing is in no way enjoyable, particularly when it implies forfeiting something critical to you. For instance, on the off chance that you settle on some unacceptable choice, your work, your connections, your bliss, or even your life could be in question.

In certain choices, you know what the result will be immediate, it's obvious. For instance, you're attempting to choose if you will go to work today. Assuming you decide to go, you're going to get compensated. Assuming not, you're not going to get compensated.

Nonetheless, for certain choices, the result will not be known until a certain period has passed. For instance, you've put resources into your companion's business. You realize your companion has some business-wise, however you won't discover until months or even a long time later if your speculation was an insightful choice.

Anyway, how would you realize you're settling on the best decision throughout everyday life? Here are 3 signs you're settling on the right decision:

Your instincts say it's the right choice

You've most likely settled on choices before were somewhere inside you realize you're making the best choice (even though your brain says you're committing an error). Also, it worked out that you were correct! By and large, you most likely didn't have the foggiest idea why you settled on that decision, you simply realize that somewhere down in your heart it was the right call.

Some odd individuals might say it was your divine messenger or some higher, imperceptible power instructing you. Be that as it may, for those who trust in science, they say it's a mix of past encounters and information. Our cerebrums some way or another associate the spots and decipher the information to instruct us.

There are innumerable accounts of individuals who've paid attention to their instinct and lived to tell about it. They've some way or another figured out how to keep away from mishaps, catastrophes, liquidations, and other similar life-changing (or life-finishing) occasions. Thus, assuming you're confronted with a troublesome choice at this moment, take a stab at paying attention to what your stomach says.

You're proud of your decision

Assuming your choice is something you can live with, then, at that point, it's a decent sign you've settled on the best decision. Yet, assuming you will be embarrassed about it, then, at that point, clearly it's some unacceptable one. Here is a model: you wind up drawn to somebody, yet you realize they're now hitched, and this individual likewise admitted they feel the same way about you. Would it be advisable for you to seek after the relationship or not? Assuming you can live with demolishing somebody's marriage, then, at that point, that is your decision. In any case, if your ethics and your qualities let you know that doing as such is off-base, then, at that point, you want to make the best decision. Eventually, you'll be glad for yourself. You can rest adequately around evening time realizing you didn't cheat and obliterate your marriage.

You've gauged the pros and cons

Critical choices need examination. At times, paying attention to your stomach nature most likely won't help you. For instance, moving to another nation is anything but something seemingly insignificant. Leaving all that natural behind can't be simple. In any case, you realize that there's a superior chance sitting tight for you abroad.

Your stomach intuition will likely advise you to remain, yet your rationale may advise you to take the plunge. In any event, record the upsides and downsides of every choice. Then, at that point, sit on it for a couple of days and return to it when you've thoroughly considered things.

Eventually, what's significant is that you pursue what's going to satisfy you. You might ask others for their feedback, however, keep in mind, it's your life, and your activities will affect you more than any other person.

Chapter 10

Paying It Forward

"When you're in a position that you can comfortably give, you need to pay it forward." - Nelsan Ellis

Paying it forward simply means doing the same favor you've received from someone else to other people. For instance, someone did a small, kind favor for you today. Instead of paying back that person, you do the same kind of favor to someone else. Paying it forward is a very powerful concept. One random act of kindness has the power to change someone's day for the better. Imagine if everyone in the whole world practiced this concept. One good deed can touch billions of people!

While we can only dream about living in a much better world, paying it forward can truly make a lot of people's lives better. Your generosity and your kindness are going to make others happy. But will it make you happy as well?

Well, research says yes. Giving makes you feel good about yourself. You may have hurt a lot of people in the past, but when you do a good deed for a stranger, you think there may be hope for you yet. It gives you a rush that's unlike any other. It makes you feel fantastic you did something that helped somebody, and made them happy in the process!

Being kind has a lot of tangible benefits. Here are some of the top ones:

It makes us happy

Certain people say thought is misrepresented because it sets you up as a conspicuous target for abuse. This may be substantial, but by then again, no standard book says you should be kind to everyone. Few out of every odd individual merit your mindfulness. The subsequent you feel like you're being taken advantage of, just proceed from that person.

Do whatever it takes not to permit several ruined eggs to redirect you off from aiding others. There are abundance more people who will see the worth in your help and will be

eager to pay your thoughtfulness forward. These are individuals you ought to endeavor to assist.

All things considered, when you assist with people who genuinely need your assistance, you'll feel a profound feeling of bliss and achievement that you're not going to find elsewhere.

It improves relationships

We normally incline toward individuals who ooze inspiration, that incorporates individuals we view to be great and kind. While it's actual you should just assistance somebody since you need to help, not because you're anticipating anything consequently, the reality stays that being caring has a couple of side advantages.

These incorporate causing others to feel 'near' you. They'd feel like you're a close friend, somebody who comprehends their battles and will assist them with excursion in hardship.

Regardless of how furious or vexed you might be at somebody assuming they carry out something to be thankful for that benefits you, it, at last, makes it more straightforward for you to 'pardon' them. So, consideration can repair and further develop connections.

It improves our lives

Have a go at doing an arbitrary thoughtful gesture each day for half a month, and check whether that doesn't transform into a beneficial routine. At the point when you've made thoughtfulness a propensity, your smugness will be at an untouched high.

Individuals whose lives you've contacted in some little manner will be appreciative to you. You'll make new companions. You'll be more joyful. You'll be a more sure individual. You'll be a delight to be around with.

However, anticipate nothing consequently. Assuming individuals you've assisted proceed with showing proactive kindness, you're making your local area – and the world - a vastly improved spot.

Regardless of how little or unimportant you think your thoughtful gesture is, keep doing it. You may not know it, however, this large number of little things will add up, and your consideration will return to you when you wouldn't dare hope anymore. It's the way karma and the universe works.

Conclusion

Final Conclusion

Your joy starts with you. Assuming that you're in a despondent state at this moment, look profound inside you for replies. Sort out why you're despondent and from that point, investigate working on yourself and building more certain associations with others.

Figure out how to cherish yourself and fulfill yourself first. It's going to be hard fulfilling others assuming that you can't be cheerful yourself. Settle on the ideal decisions and the ideal choices. Start by supplanting your negative propensities with positive ones. Fulfill a work to be what's more figure out how to keep up with that joy despite preliminaries and afflictions – your street to 'joyfully at any point after' has quite recently started.

www.ingramcontent.com/pod-product-compliance
Lightning Source LLC
LaVergne TN
LVHW050421160726
843469LV00041B/1181

* 9 7 8 9 3 5 5 5 9 0 4 8 0 *